DRAWING WITH
Circles

GODELEINE DE ROSAMEL

Gareth Stevens Publishing
A WORLD ALMANAC EDUCATION GROUP COMPANY

Please visit our web site at: www.garethstevens.com
For a free color catalog describing Gareth Stevens Publishing's list
of high-quality books and multimedia programs, call 1-800-542-2595 (USA) or
1-800-387-3178 (Canada). Gareth Stevens Publishing's fax: (414) 332-3567.

Library of Congress Cataloging-in-Publication Data

De Rosamel, Godeleine.
        [Dessine avec des ronds. English]
        Drawing with circles/by Godeleine De Rosamel.
            p. cm. — (Drawing is easy)
        Summary: Step-by-step illustrations demonstrate how to use circles as the
starting point for drawings.
        Includes bibliographical references.
        ISBN 0-8368-3625-1 (lib. bdg.)
        1. Drawing—Technique—Juvenile literature.   2. Circle in art—Juvenile
literature. [1. Drawing—Technique.] I. Title.
NC655.R668313   2003
741.2—dc21   2002036538

This edition first published in 2003 by
Gareth Stevens Publishing
A World Almanac Education Group Company
330 West Olive Street, Suite 100
Milwaukee, WI 53212 USA

This edition © 2003 by Gareth Stevens, Inc.
First published as *Dessine: Avec des ronds* in 2000 by Editions Casterman.
© 2000 by Casterman. Additional end matter © 2003 by Gareth Stevens, Inc.

Translation: Patrice Lantier
Gareth Stevens editor: Dorothy L. Gibbs
Gareth Stevens designer: Melissa Valuch
Cover design: Melissa Valuch

Printed in the United States of America

1 2 3 4 5 6 7 8 9 07 06 05 04 03

Table of Contents

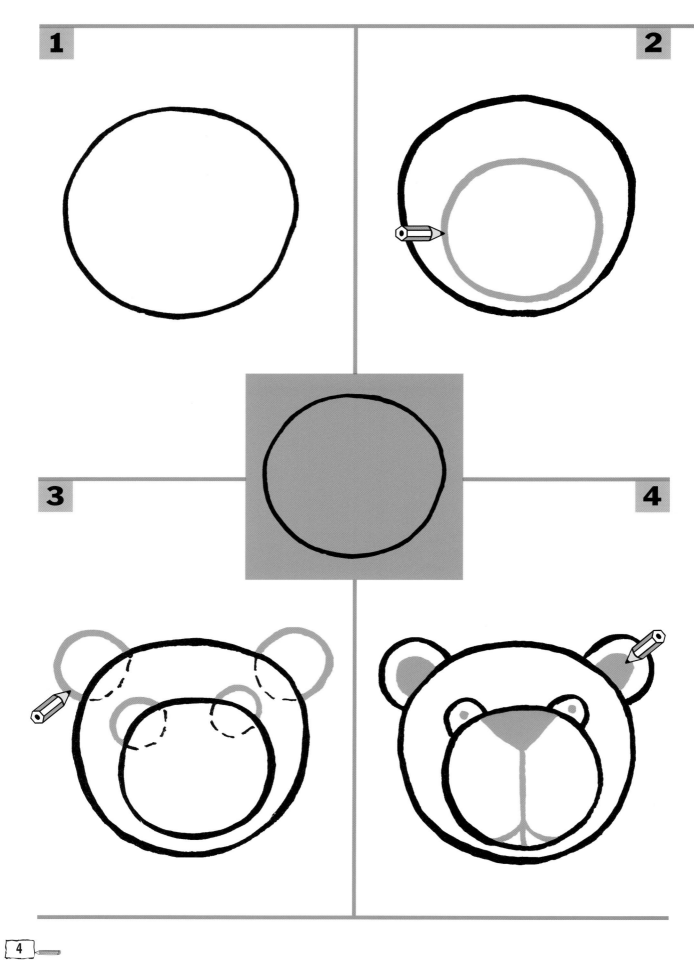

a bear

a dog   a cat   a koala   a mouse

a hippopotamus

a cow   a reindeer   a bull

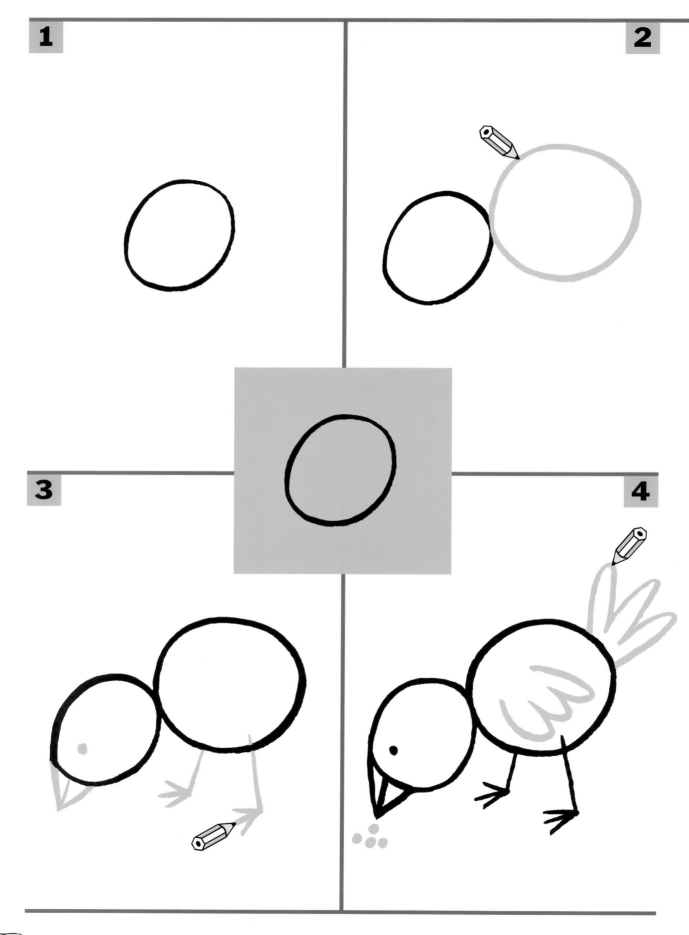

a bird

a bird walking | **a bird flying** | **a duck** | **a chicken**

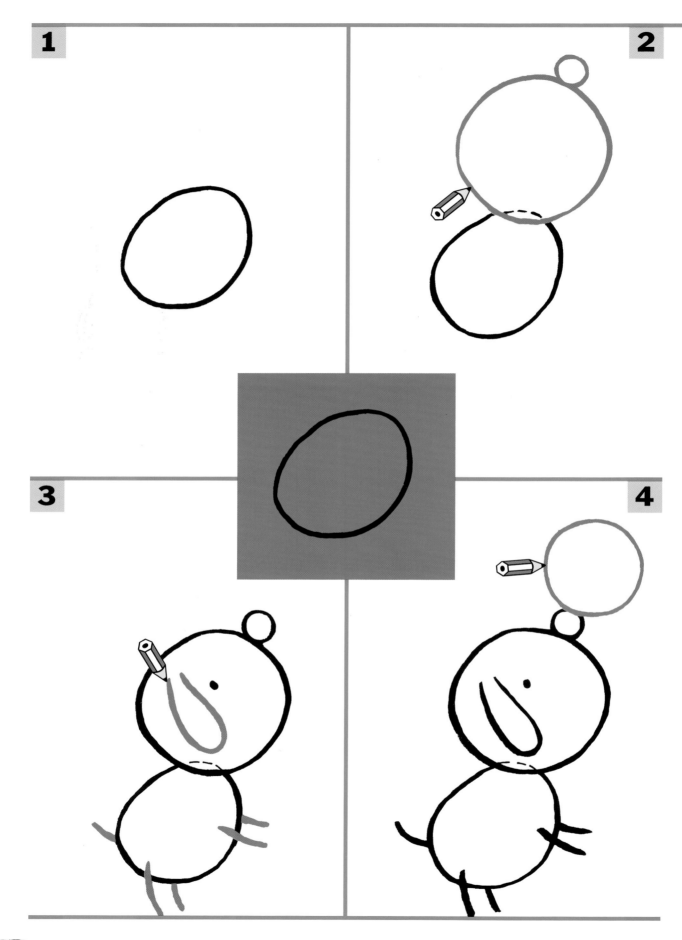

a puppy

a puppy running | a puppy face | a puppy sitting

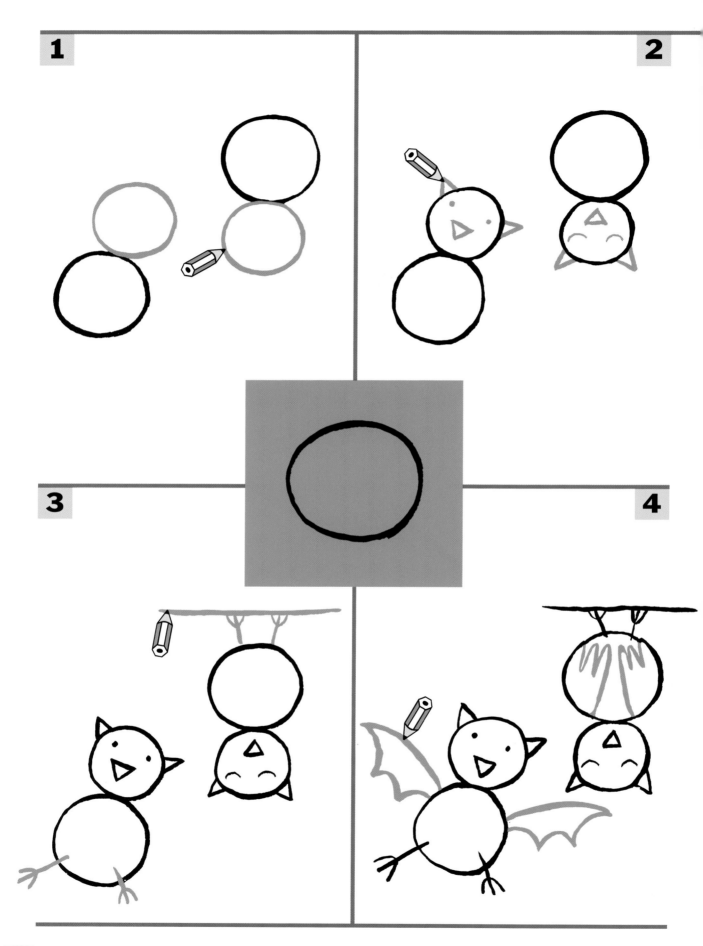

1 **2**

3 **4**

two bats

| an owl | a rabbit | a cat | a squirrel |

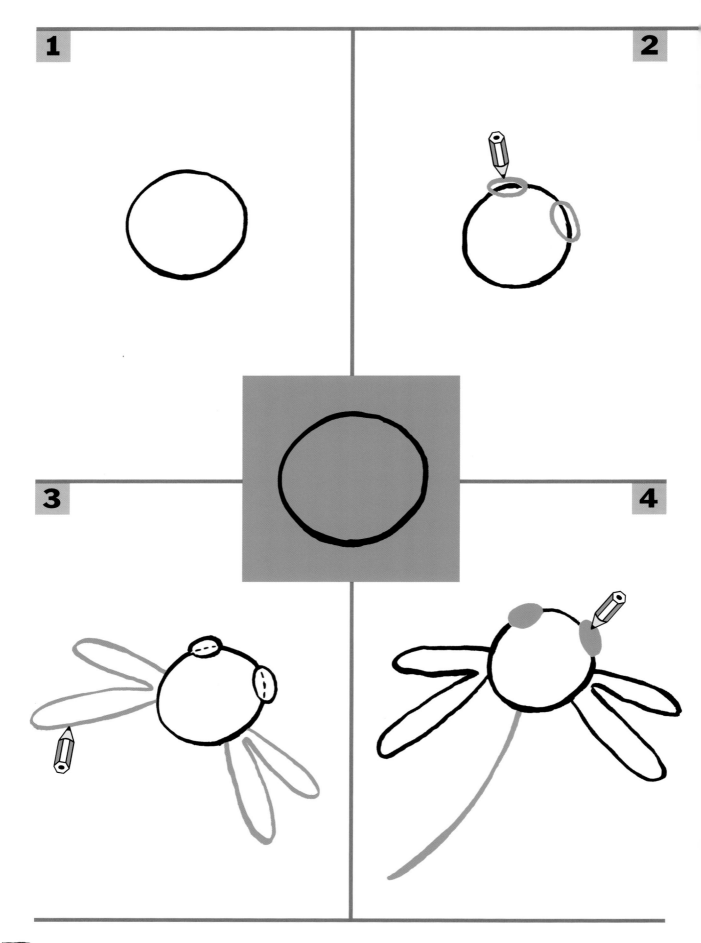

a dragonfly

a butterfly | **a ladybug** | **a spider**

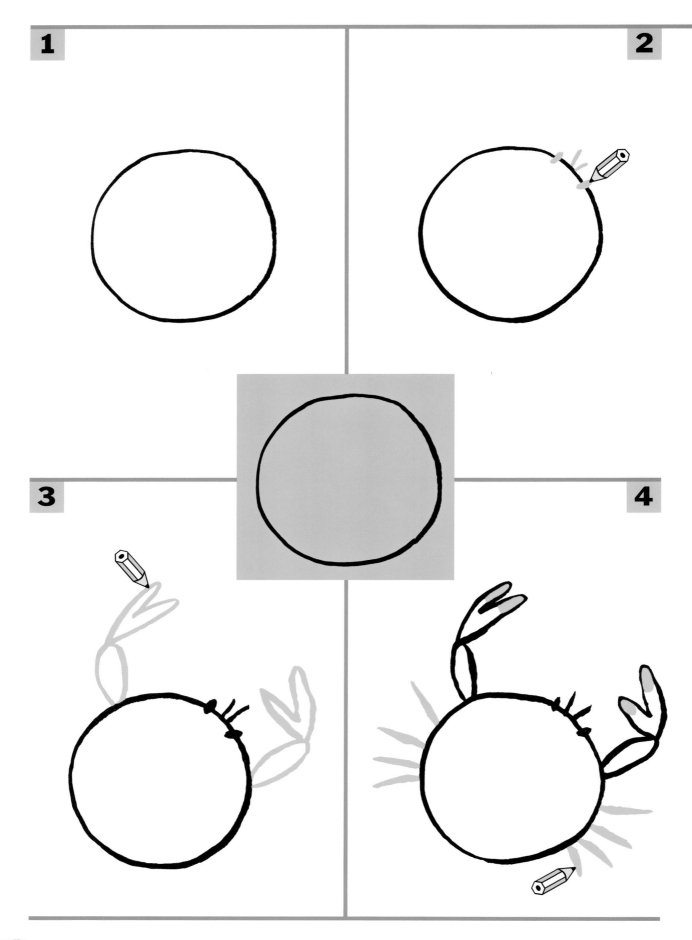

a crab

a hedgehog   **a mouse**   **a frog**

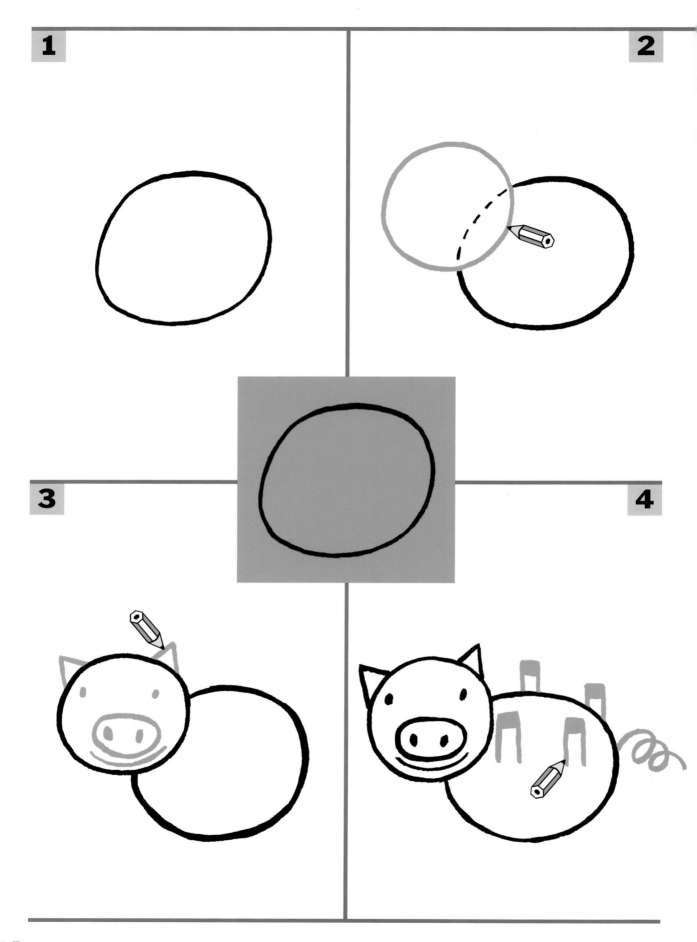

1

2

3

4

a pig

a happy pig

a pig doing tricks

a pig walking

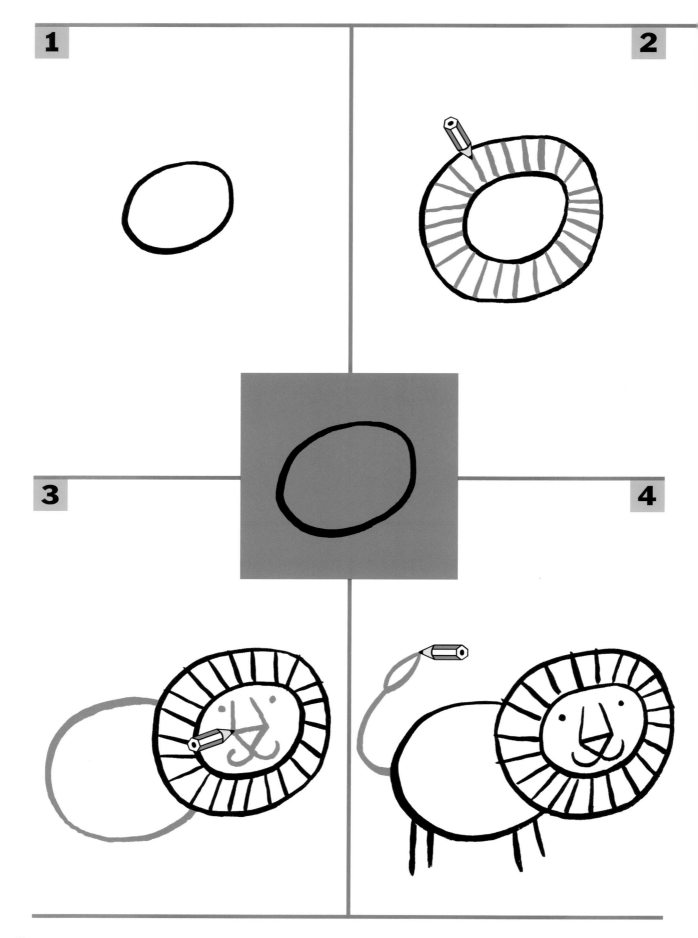

a lion cub

a mother lion

a curly lion

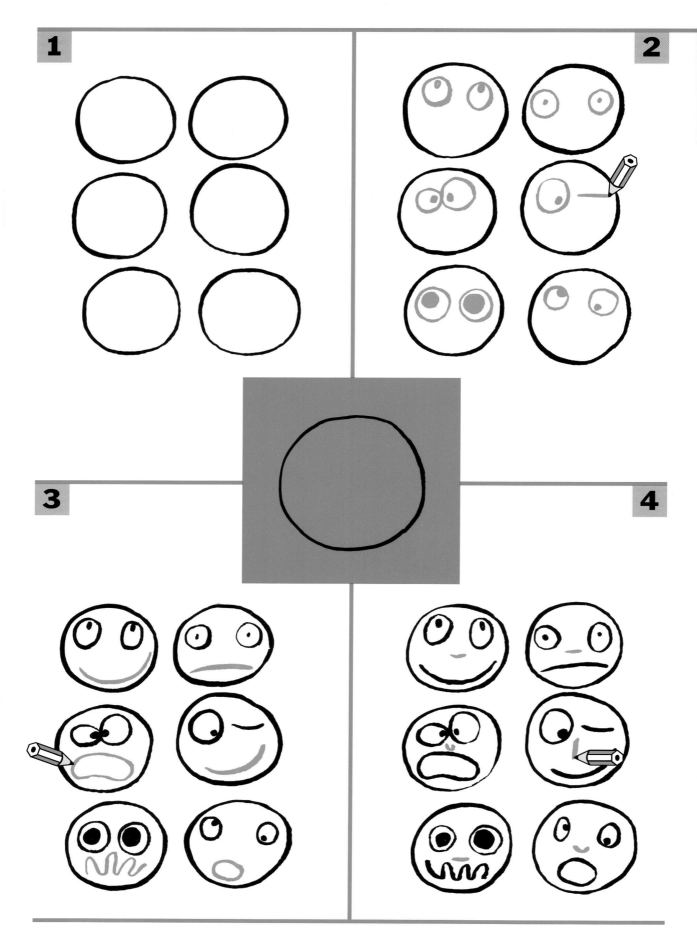

silly faces

| a baby face | curly hair | eyeglasses | a clown face |

more drawing books

- *Bob the Builder: Draw the Team*
  Ian Hillyard
  (Golden Books)

- *Ed Emberley's Picture Pie: A Circle Drawing Book*
  Ed Emberley
  (Econo-Clad Books)

- *I Can Draw Wild Animals. I Can Draw Animals* (series)
  Hélène Leroux-Hugon
  (Gareth Stevens)

web sites

- Sesame Street® Coloring Pages: Shapes
  www.sesameworkshop.org/sesamestreet/coloringpages/

- The SunShine Room: Let's Play with Shapes!
  akidsheart.com/threer/lvl1/shapes.htm